The
WINTER
SOLSTICE

Library of Congress Cataloging-in-Publication Data
Jackson, Ellen B., 1943–
The winter solstice / by Ellen Jackson
illustrated by Jan Davey Ellis.
p.   cm.
Includes bibliographical references and index.
Summary: Presents facts and folklore about the shortest day of the
year, a day that has been filled with magic since ancient times.
ISBN 1-56294-400-2 (lib. bdg.)
ISBN 0-7613-0297-2 (pbk.)

1. Winter solstice—Juvenile literature. [1. Winter solstice.]
I. Ellis, Jan Davey, ill. II. Title.
GT4995.W55J33   1994
394.2′683—dc20   92-45065   CIP   AC

Published by The Millbrook Press
2 Old New Milford Road, Brookfield, Connecticut 06804

First paperback edition published in 1997

The
WINTER
SOLSTICE

BY ELLEN JACKSON

ILLUSTRATED BY
JAN DAVEY ELLIS

The Millbrook Press ✳ Brookfield, Connecticut

Long ago,
on one of the shortest days of the year,
a Scottish family huddled by a fire. Outside,
the winds raged and howled in the gathering gloom.

The family believed that trolls and evil spirits walked
the Earth during late fall and early winter, when the
sun was at its lowest point in the sky. But the father
knew a Scottish ritual that would keep the family safe.

He took three glowing coals from the fire and
dropped them into a basin of water. Then each
family member washed with the special water.
They believed that the magic of fire and water
together would protect them from evil spirits.

Hundreds of years ago, many people, like this Scottish family, thought that ghosts and witches and trolls wandered the Earth. One especially dangerous time was the winter solstice, the first day of winter. On this day darkness comes earlier than at any other time of the year, and the sun is at its lowest point in the sky.

People worried that the sun's strength would not return. Without the sun's light there could be no plants, no animals, no humans.

With evil spirits everywhere, neighbors had to join forces. This was a time for goodwill, forgiveness, and love. Many ancient people believed that special rituals and ceremonies could help the sun be reborn. In some places animals or even humans were sacrificed at the solstice. Priests dressed as animals or birds danced and chanted. They believed each detail of the ceremony had to be right for the next harvest to be good.

Thousands of years ago, at Stonehenge and other places in the British Isles, people placed huge stones together to frame the setting sun on the day of the winter solstice. As the red sun sank slowly in the west, the last rays of light gleamed through a special space between the stones. These people wanted to know when the sun would regain its strength, and they went to great trouble to mark the exact time this would happen.

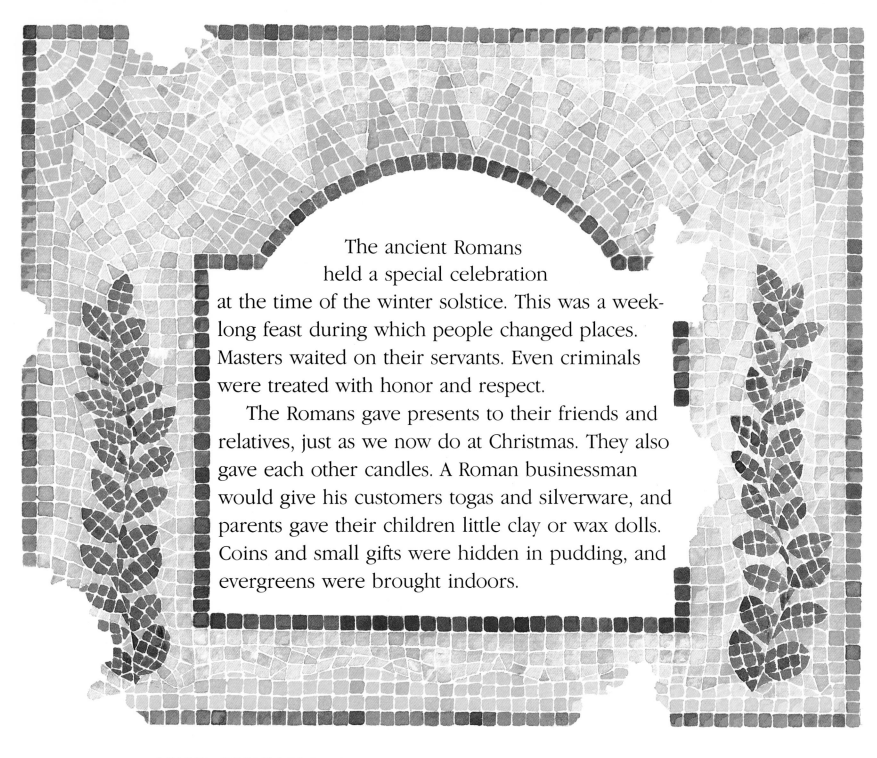

The ancient Romans held a special celebration at the time of the winter solstice. This was a week-long feast during which people changed places. Masters waited on their servants. Even criminals were treated with honor and respect.

The Romans gave presents to their friends and relatives, just as we now do at Christmas. They also gave each other candles. A Roman businessman would give his customers togas and silverware, and parents gave their children little clay or wax dolls. Coins and small gifts were hidden in pudding, and evergreens were brought indoors.

In the far north, the sun disappeared for many days. After thirty-five days without light, the Scandinavians sent scouts to the mountaintops to look for the sun's return. When the first glimmer of light was spotted, the scouts returned with the good news. A great festival, the feast of Yuletide, began.

During this feast, men (not the women) sat in a long hall shaped like a boat and feasted around the fire while the crackling Yule log burned. The main dish was often the head of a wild boar, which was roasted with a fruit in its mouth.

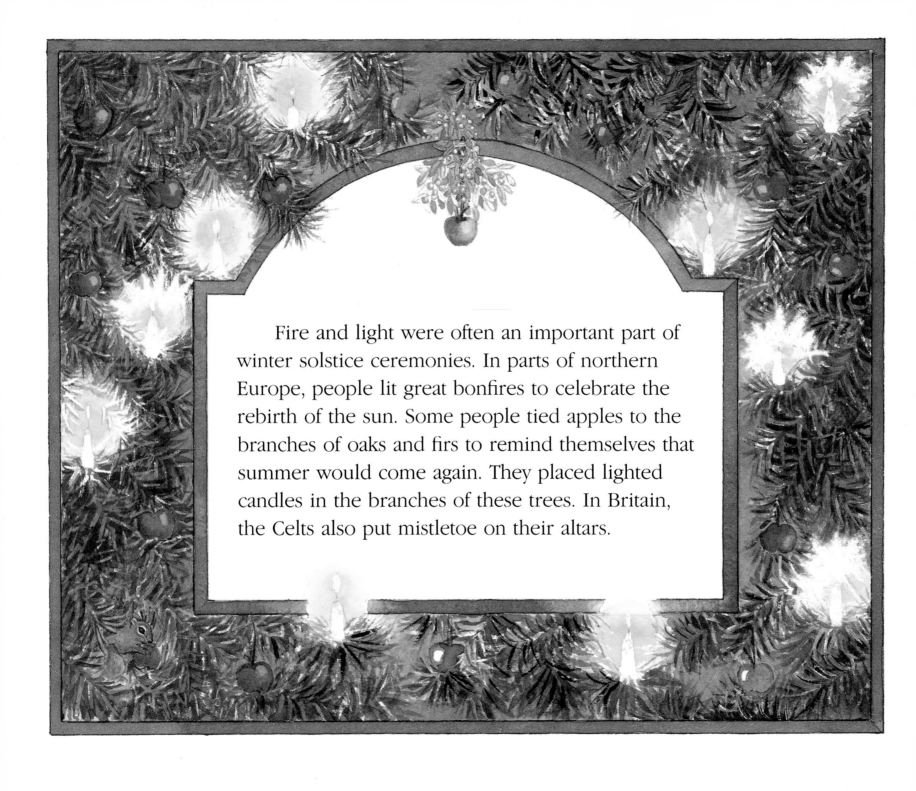

Fire and light were often an important part of winter solstice ceremonies. In parts of northern Europe, people lit great bonfires to celebrate the rebirth of the sun. Some people tied apples to the branches of oaks and firs to remind themselves that summer would come again. They placed lighted candles in the branches of these trees. In Britain, the Celts also put mistletoe on their altars.

In Peru, the Indians performed four sun festivals during the year. The most important of these was the winter solstice festival. For three days the Indians ate no food. On the fourth day, everyone gathered in the public square before dawn to await the coming of the sun.

When the sun appeared, shouts of joy rang out. The chief priest drank from a cup that was then passed to others. At the temple of the sun, a llama was sacrificed. Then the rays of the sun were focused with a mirror to make a fire. This fire was carried to all the temples, where it was kept burning on the altars throughout the year.

Other Native Americans also had special sun festivals. The Hopi and other Pueblo Indians of Arizona and New Mexico built sacred buildings called kivas. Slots in the edges of the outer walls of the kivas let in the rays of the rising and setting sun and moon throughout the year.

The ceremonies that marked the return of the sun were carried out by Hopi priests who dressed in the skins of animals. The feathers in their head-dresses were meant to look like the rays of the sun. Some of these ceremonies are still performed.

Even today, the Kwakiutl Indians of British Columbia change their names and take on the names of their ancestors at the beginning of winter. They believe that this will protect them from the spirits of the dead who return at this time of year.

People in the United States and Europe still mark the winter solstice. But for many reasons this time of year does not seem as frightening to us as it did to our ancestors.

Today, when the earth is bare and brown and the cold vanilla taste of winter is in the air, no one worries about the darkness or the whistling wind. People simply turn on the lights, pour themselves a cup of hot chocolate, and go about their business.

Scientists now know why the days grow shorter in winter. The seasons are caused by the changing position of the Earth in relation to the sun.

If you stick one toothpick in the top of an orange, and another toothpick in the bottom, you can see how the position of the Earth creates the seasons. In a dark room, shine a flashlight (which represents the sun) directly at the middle or center part of the orange (which represents the Earth). Tilt the North Pole toothpick slightly toward the light. You will see that most of the light shines on the top part of the orange.

This is the position of the sun and Earth during the Northern Hemisphere's summer. Now tilt the North Pole slightly away from the light. This is the position of the Earth at the time of the Northern Hemisphere's winter solstice, when it receives less sunlight than the Southern Hemisphere. People living in the tropics, near the equator, do not have true seasons. There, the amount of light is always about the same, and the temperature is always warm.

How do we celebrate the winter solstice today? You may have noticed that many of the things we do at Christmas and Hanukkah come from winter solstice rituals of long ago.

Like the Romans, we light candles, give gifts to our friends and relatives, and make special foods and desserts. Like the people of northern Europe long ago, we decorate a tree and hang mistletoe. Like many ancient people, we celebrate the season as a time of love and goodwill.

The winter solstice is still, for us, a new beginning. It's a time to hope that darkness will give way to light and that the world will be a better place in the year to come.

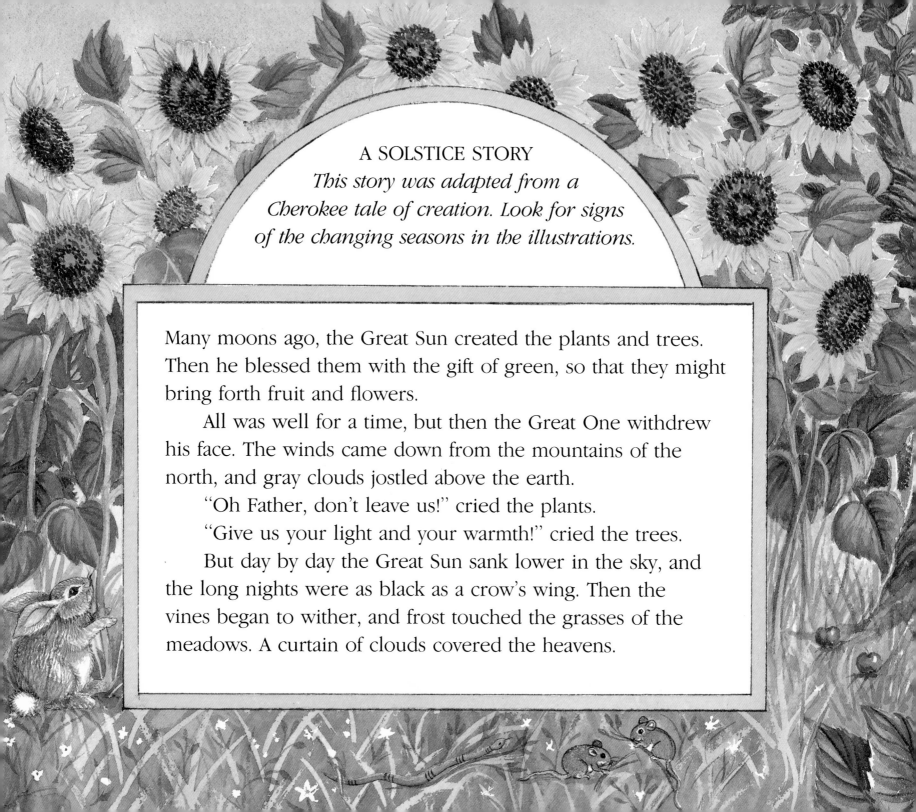

A SOLSTICE STORY
*This story was adapted from a
Cherokee tale of creation. Look for signs
of the changing seasons in the illustrations.*

Many moons ago, the Great Sun created the plants and trees.
Then he blessed them with the gift of green, so that they might
bring forth fruit and flowers.

All was well for a time, but then the Great One withdrew
his face. The winds came down from the mountains of the
north, and gray clouds jostled above the earth.

"Oh Father, don't leave us!" cried the plants.

"Give us your light and your warmth!" cried the trees.

But day by day the Great Sun sank lower in the sky, and
the long nights were as black as a crow's wing. Then the
vines began to wither, and frost touched the grasses of the
meadows. A curtain of clouds covered the heavens.

"Dear Father, we will die without you," wailed the trees and plants. "Come back! Come back!"

"He's coming," whispered the North Wind. "There's a touch of gold on the mountaintops."

"He's coming," whispered the clouds. "His face has turned in the sky."

The plants and trees were full of joy at the good news. Eager to greet their dear father, they decided to stay awake every night and watch for his return.

Sumac, sassafras, and purple aster put forth brilliant colors to welcome the Great Sun. But after a night of watching, they fell asleep.

The dogwoods and alders watched for two nights, but soon their boughs grew heavy and they, too, fell asleep.

The maples and poplars whispered to each other, "We will not give in to sleep." But soon they were slumbering under the cold stars like the others.

When the Great Sun came from his wigwam on the dawn of the seventh day, the skies were clear. He looked down on the forests and meadows below. The only plants and trees still awake to greet him were the pine, the fir, the spruce, the holly, and the laurel.

"For your faithfulness I will give you the gift of green forever," said the Great Sun to the plants and trees who welcomed him. "The others will drop their leaves or sleep through the winter, but you will remain awake. Your color will be a promise of my return to all who see you."

And he sent a stream of light across the sleeping earth.

ABOUT THE AUTHOR AND ILLUSTRATOR:

Author Ellen Jackson has written more than half a dozen picture books for children, including *Ants Can't Dance* and *Boris the Boring Boar,* as well as nonfiction books on subjects that range from crime prevention to earthquake safety. A former elementary-school teacher who now writes full-time, she lives in Santa Barbara, California, where she enjoys exploring tide pools along the shore.

Columbus, Ohio, artist Jan Davey Ellis's illustration credits include two books for The Millbrook Press: *Mush! Across Alaska in the World's Longest Sled-Dog Race,* by Patricia Seibert, and *Fiesta! Mexico's Great Celebrations,* by Elizabeth Silverthorne. Both were named Notable Children's Trade Books in the Field of Social Studies by the National Council for the Social Studies and the Children's Book Council.